MarcoPolo

HIS NOTEBOOK

by Susan L. Roth

DOUBLEDAY

New York   London   Toronto   Sydney   Auckland

I would like to thank Mariangela Aloj, Mary Cash, Margaret Coughlan, Susan E. Davis, Thomas G. DeClaire, Laveta Emory, Meg Grasselli, Raymond Hebert, George Hobart, Helen and John Kang, Kay Kenyon, Lily Kesckes, Charles Rand, Harry Rutstein of the Marco Polo Foundation, Inc., Janet Vultee, and Jennifer Yohalem.

The following institutions have graciously granted permission to reproduce prints, photographs, and maps from their collections:

The Library of Congress, Geography and Maps Division (pp. 3, 4, 5, 9, 13, 26, and 31). The Library of Congress, Prints and Photographs Division (front cover, pp. 7, 10, 14, 22, 25, 29, and 32). The National Gallery of Art, Print Study Room, Washington, D.C. (back cover: B-2627 *The Lion of St. Mark*, c. 1490, Martin Schongauer, c. 1450–91; p. 12: detail from B-3126 *Adoration of the Magi*, c. 1400–30, Anonymous German Painter, Fifteenth Century, Rosewald Collection; p. 20: detail from B-11165 *Elephant*; p. 27: detail from *Man Seated by a Palm Tree*, c. 1510–11, Benedetto Montagna, c. 1481–1558, Rosewald Collection). The Smithsonian Institution, Washington, D.C., Division of Numismatics (p. 16). The Smithsonian Institution, The Freer Gallery of Art, Washington, D.C. (p. 19: detail from 11.209 Chinese Painting, early Ming Dynasty [Fourteenth–Fifteenth Century], *Panorama of West Lake Hang Chou*). The Smithsonian Institution Libraries, National Zoological Park Branch, Washington, D.C. (p. 24). The Textile Museum, Washington, D.C. (p. 18: 3.282).

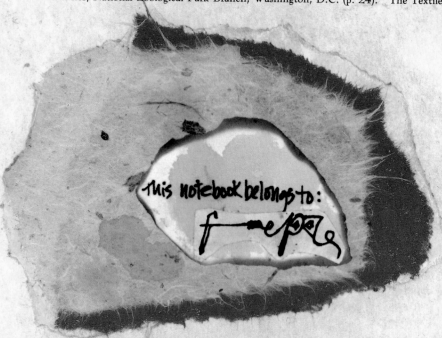

This notebook belongs to: f nepole

Published by Doubleday   a division of Bantam Doubleday Dell Publishing Group, Inc.   666 Fifth Avenue, New York, New York 10103   Doubleday and the portrayal of an anchor with a dolphin are trademarks of Doubleday, a division of Bantam Doubleday Dell Publishing Group, Inc.   *Designed by Richard Oriolo*
Library of Congress Cataloging-in-Publication Data   Roth, Susan L.   Marco Polo: His Notebook / Susan Roth.—1st ed.   p.   cm.   Summary: Marco Polo's travels are recorded in an authentic-looking diary and scrapbook such as the great explorer might have kept.   1. Polo, Marco, 1254–1323?—Journeys—Juvenile literature. 2. Voyages and travels—Juvenile literature.   3. Explorers—Italy—Biography—Juvenile literature.   4. China—Description and travel—To 1900—Juvenile literature. [1. Polo, Marco, 1254–1323?   2. Explorers.   3. Voyages and travels.]   I. Title.   G370.P9R68 1990   910.92—dc20   [92] 89-23619 CIP   AC   ISBN 0-385-26495-X   ISBN 0-385-26555-7 (lib. bdg.)   RL:3.1   Copyright © 1990 by Susan L. Roth   All Rights Reserved
Printed in Hong Kong   February 1991   First Edition in the United States of America

For Henue and Unc. Johnny
with love and in appreciation of my
first geography lessons.

—SWLR

*T*his is not a true story, although it could have been. It is based on Marco Polo's own book *The Travels of Marco Polo,* and on many scholarly works about him, written over the last seven hundred years. No one is certain of the real story. Scholars began arguing about Marco Polo and his travels as soon as the book was completed. Some contemporary scholars are still arguing.

There are many reasons for these disputes. Seven hundred years ago, travel and communication were so difficult that most Europeans knew nothing about distant lands. Few people traveled. Books were rare because they had to be hand-copied, not printed. Most people could not read. There were no newspapers, radios, televisions, telephones, or cameras.

Besides this, many ordinary aspects of Chinese life seemed extraordinary to Europeans. The postal system, coal, and paper money were incredible to Marco Polo but incomprehensible to people who had merely heard about these things.

In his day, Marco Polo earned the nickname "il Milione," which means the million, probably because of his stories about the riches of the Mongol ruler of Asia and the wonders of faraway places. Many thought he spoke of things too grand to be true.

Even when *The Travels of Marco Polo* appeared, most people didn't believe Marco Polo's wild stories. It became a common expression to say "That's a Marco Polo" when someone was exaggerating or obviously lying.

It is known that Marco Polo included some of his descriptions of exotic things and exotic places only because he had heard stories about them. It is not always clear if his experience is a first- or a second-hand one. Only in some cases have scholars been able to determine what is fact.

For example, although Marco Polo speaks about Madagascar as though he had been there, it is a known fact that he never went there. The same is true for the segment which he wrote on Japan. If one reads this part carefully, then one sees that he does not admit to having been there.

There is also the mystery of the Great Wall. It is very hard to believe that in his China travels Marco Polo never saw it. Yet he does not mention it. Some extremists argue that this is reason enough to think that Marco Polo never went to China at all. In spite of conflicting opinions, it is now believed that most of Marco Polo's story is true.

In this book I have told only Marco Polo's own story. This book is based upon his book.

I have created what I imagine might remain of his original travel journals, Marco Polo's own notebook, the notebook on which he based his description of the world.

Most of this story is also true, so let's pretend the rest together.

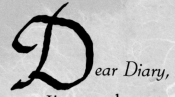ear Diary,

I'm standing on the deck of our ship, memorizing the beautiful church of San Marco, the pillars, and the pink and yellow buildings lining the canals of Venice.

Good-bye to the gondoliers! Good-bye to the crowds on the docks, my family, and my friends. My Venetian world looks smaller and paler as we sail farther out to sea.

I'm seventeen years old. Will I be twenty when I return? Who knows! Uncle Maffeo says we might *never* get home. But Papa says of course we will but that in our eyes Venice will never look quite the same again.

I don't have to say good-bye to our Venetian lion, though. He waves on our flag, red and gold and proud, high on our masts. A little bit of Venice will always be with us.

Without Papa and Uncle Maffeo with me, I might not sound so brave. But we are the Polo family, and we are strong together. I turn my head to the gray ocean and I don't look back again.

Our journey has begun.

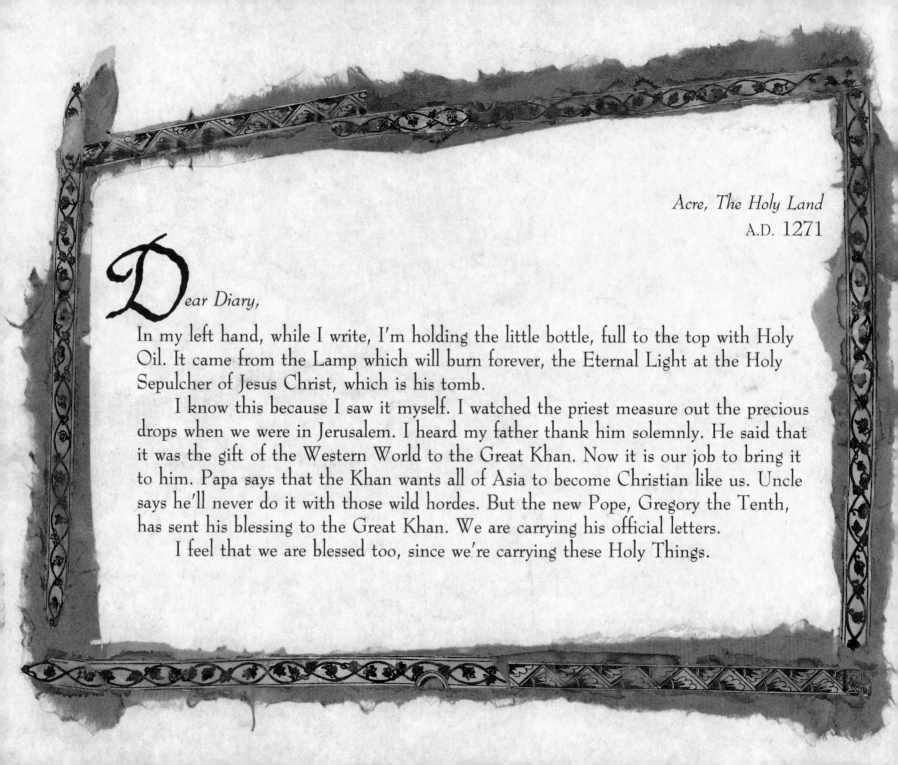

Acre, The Holy Land
A.D. 1271

*D*ear Diary,

In my left hand, while I write, I'm holding the little bottle, full to the top with Holy Oil. It came from the Lamp which will burn forever, the Eternal Light at the Holy Sepulcher of Jesus Christ, which is his tomb.

I know this because I saw it myself. I watched the priest measure out the precious drops when we were in Jerusalem. I heard my father thank him solemnly. He said that it was the gift of the Western World to the Great Khan. Now it is our job to bring it to him. Papa says that the Khan wants all of Asia to become Christian like us. Uncle says he'll never do it with those wild hordes. But the new Pope, Gregory the Tenth, has sent his blessing to the Great Khan. We are carrying his official letters.

I feel that we are blessed too, since we're carrying these Holy Things.

s V. M.   100   *Via Bethlehem*   26   36   114

50   *Castrum Pisanum*   24   115   113

42   31   25   98   97

20   32   23   21   22   19   27   37

18

41   16   15

5   13

4   12

3   2   9

40   39

62

Vallis Iosaphat 57   *Gethsemani Villa* 54

Torrens Cedron 52   56   63

77   73   58   *Sepulchrum B. M. V.* 64

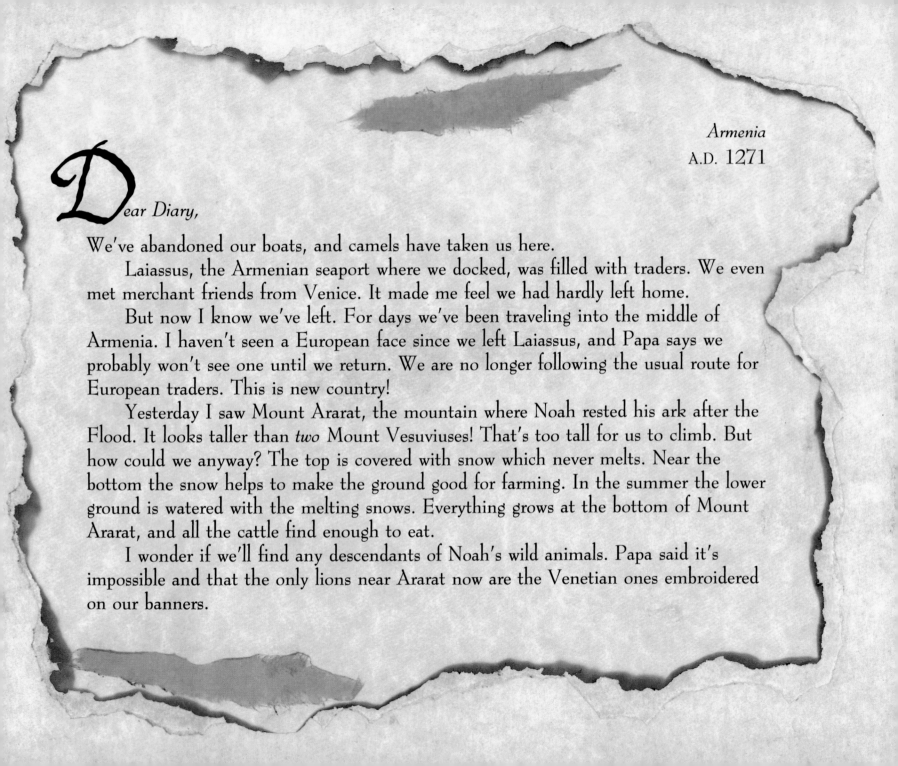

*D*ear Diary,

We've abandoned our boats, and camels have taken us here.

Laiassus, the Armenian seaport where we docked, was filled with traders. We even met merchant friends from Venice. It made me feel we had hardly left home.

But now I know we've left. For days we've been traveling into the middle of Armenia. I haven't seen a European face since we left Laiassus, and Papa says we probably won't see one until we return. We are no longer following the usual route for European traders. This is new country!

Yesterday I saw Mount Ararat, the mountain where Noah rested his ark after the Flood. It looks taller than *two* Mount Vesuviuses! That's too tall for us to climb. But how could we anyway? The top is covered with snow which never melts. Near the bottom the snow helps to make the ground good for farming. In the summer the lower ground is watered with the melting snows. Everything grows at the bottom of Mount Ararat, and all the cattle find enough to eat.

I wonder if we'll find any descendants of Noah's wild animals. Papa said it's impossible and that the only lions near Ararat now are the Venetian ones embroidered on our banners.

*D*ear Diary,

There are Fire-Worshippers in Persia!

We are stopping here in the city of Saba, the home of the Three Wise Men.

Nearby Saba is a castle called Cala Ataperistan, Castle of the Fire-Worshippers. The people here really are just that. They have been since the time of the Three Wise Men. This is why:

When the wise men left Bethlehem, Jesus gave them a box which they were to bring home unopened. But one wise man became curious and opened it up once they were near Saba. Inside was a stone to remind them to keep their Christian faith firm like a stone.

But another of the wise men decided it was a trick. He angrily lifted the rock from the box and hurled it into a big pit. As soon as the rock touched the bottom, the whole pit filled with flames. The fire would not go out.

The wise men were ashamed that they had doubted Jesus. One caught some of the fire on a stick and carried it home to Saba. They placed the fire in a chapel. The fire has been burning ever since. The townspeople worship and pray to the fire as if the flames themselves were God.

ear Diary,

This is the day we have been waiting for. It has taken us almost a year to prepare to cross this great desert, which the Mongols call the Gobi. At last we have come to it.

We have stocked enough food for forty days. Uncle Maffeo says it will take that long for us to cross. The first city on the other side is Karkoran, and we have to take care of ourselves until we get there. We probably won't meet another human being the whole time.

The camels took long drinks of water. That should last them for *two* deserts, Papa joked.

This desert is not as I imagined it. There's no sand! It is made of thousands and thousands of tiny gray pebbles.

It's gray, empty, still, and endless.

We have thirty-nine days to go.

Dear Diary,

At last we have arrived at the Great Khan's palace! He even sent us a welcoming escort for the last forty days of our journey.

But how do you suppose that the Khan knew that we were forty days from Shangdu? It seemed like magic to me, but now I know he has a post system. What's a post system? It's amazing, that's what it is.

The Khan has the fastest horses in the world. They move much faster than our camels. He also has skilled riders. Each rider is waiting at a set location, ready to travel quickly between two places carrying messages. It's like a giant relay race and with so many horses and riders, neither horses nor men get too tired. This post system brought news of our arrival to the Great Khan in Shangdu, even though we were forty days away.

Now after three and a half years we've finally reached the Khan. That's a long time to travel! The winters have been fierce. But the generous Khan made these past forty days into a vacation. His men took care of everything for us.

Nothing could prepare us for this magnificent palace! It is huge and built of marble and decorated with gold. Inside the gates is a private park. There is a royal pavilion, a light, open building with a huge colonnade. The roofs are made of well-varnished bamboo which are impervious to rain. The roofs are tied onto the buildings with silken cords. The structures are so light that the entire pavilion can be taken down like a tent, and set up at any other location which might please the great Khan.

The Khan has met with us and I do like him. I even think that he likes me! I'm going to study his languages so that we can really communicate.

What a palace! What richness! What beauty! What a Great Khan!

 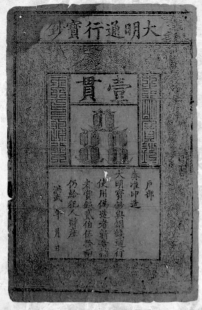 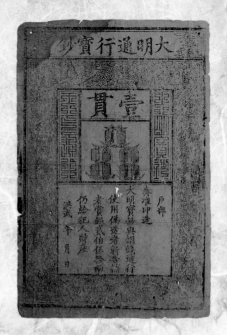

Dear Diary,

The Great Khan is a genius. He has thought of everything. Look at this. A thin, clothlike piece with some writing on it, right? Well, look again. This is money. Paper money.

The people who work for the Khan are paid with this paper, and they can use it to buy things. Even foreigners use it, because when they leave the empire, the paper can be redeemed for gold or other valuables.

The paper is made from a thin piece of mulberry tree found between the outer bark and the wooden trunk. It's pounded into paper and cut to size. Each piece is signed by designated officers. Then the Khan personally stamps each one with his seal. Making false money is a serious offense!

A bag of paper money is lighter than a bag of gold coins! It's worth more, too!

Dear Diary,

Speaking with the people is easy now, and very interesting. Most important of all, speaking the local languages has allowed me to become great friends with the Khan. He has even given me a job. I help him to oversee his vast lands and report to him on what is going on.

I think that the people accept me as the Khan's ambassador, though they still look at me strangely. Why? Because my skin is so pale. All the people here have yellow skin and slanting dark eyes. Sometimes people ask me if I am ill when they see my color.

I am so proud that I can understand these peoples' questions and that I can answer in their own languages. They like to hear stories about my home. In Venice, I tell them, *everyone* is white, eyes come in many colors, and some people even have yellow hair. This is hardest for them to believe, because in China everyone's hair and eyes are black.

But it is not only I who can teach strange things to them. Listen to what they share with me! The people in China dig black stones out of the mountains here. The stuff burns better than wood. Sometimes the fires last all night. There are plenty of trees for burning here, there's really plenty of everything. But there are so many people. Each must cook and bathe. Their homes must be heated. Probably China would run out of fuel if it weren't for these amazing black stones.

The supply seems endless and the cost is so little! Only a very Great Khan could find a substance like coal and be smart enough to make use of it!

Dear Diary,

The Great Khan must think I'm responsible and not too stupid, because he has made me *governor of Yan-gui* by his own special order! It is only a three-year term, but it is an honor which I shall treasure for life.

I love Yan-gui. It's a very important city! Yan-gui rules over twenty-four smaller towns. The people work hard as traders and artisans. It is a center for military activities. All sorts of war equipment is manufactured here and millions of soldiers live here. And now I live here too!

God bless the Great Khan! I am Marco Polo and Marco Polo is the Khan's governor in Yan-gui, one of twelve such governors in all his lands!

Dear Diary,

Since my three-year term as governor of Yan-gui has been completed I have been enjoying a close friendship with the Khan. Whenever we are in Kanbalu together, we are constant companions. He sends me on missions to distant places in his vast lands, for he is getting older and long trips are difficult for him. I love the traveling. And I enjoy reporting what I learn to the Khan. And he seems fascinated by my reports.

I want to write in my dear journal everyday, but too much is happening. Will I *ever* have time to sit down to write?

I must take time to make a few notes about Kin-Sai. It means "the Celestial City," but I call it paradise. It is so grand and exciting. I go there to visit as often as possible. There are stately bridges and elegant houses. The whole city is magnificently designed. Even the people of Kin-Sai are cordial, educated, and cultured. Kin-Sai is surely one of the great cities of the world.

*D*ear Diary,

This trip to Indo-China, a land southeast of China, has been one of my longest trips for the Khan. But I don't mind at all. If the Khan hadn't sent me to Indo-China, I never would have seen all the elephants. There are thousands and thousands of them. I was there and I saw them myself. I also met the king there. I still find it hard to believe that he has 326 children! I also sat on his beautiful black furniture made from wood found in his forests. It is the blackest and shiniest wood I have ever seen.

    I think I could travel forever for the Khan!

Madagascar and Zanzibar
A.D. 1284

*D*ear Diary,

Who could resist talking on and on about the wonders of giraffes and black tigers, and people who eat the flesh of camels. I can also tell of other amazing creatures. There are giant birds called rukhs that are big enough to lift an elephant high in the air with their talons! Although I didn't see the birds, I have seen the Khan's rukh feather. Here is a picture of it. This is how big it actually is. As you see, it won't even fit on this page.

I didn't get as far as Madagascar and Zanzibar yet, but I cannot resist writing down the stories I have heard. They are so amazing.

What a world. No one will believe it when I tell them in Venice!

Kanbalu, China
A.D. 1290

*D*ear Diary,

I thought I had lost you! Just look at the date of the last time I wrote: 1284! Six years is a long time to hide on a shelf getting dusty. But I have been so busy traveling I had almost forgotten about you.

It has been fun rereading your pages. I can't believe I began writing in 1271! It seems so long ago that I was a boy leaving Venice.

Venice. I think of Venice with longing now. Even after all these years Venice is *still* my home.

Dear Diary,

I want to go home! I can't believe I am saying these words, but I really mean them. I would give two rubies as big as my eyes for one steaming cup of Italian coffee. Uncle and Papa are also homesick. After all, we've been gone more than twenty years.

The Khan has been good to all of us, especially to me, and I love him. But now I think that he loves us even more than we love him. He doesn't understand that we are homesick. We can't get home unless he permits us, because he has such tight control of his lands. To travel peacefully through his empire, we would need a passport from him, and I know he wants us to stay forever. I also know he's getting older. If he should die before we leave, we'll never ever see Venice again.

ear Diary,

A miracle has happened! We will be able to go home!

The Khan's nephew, King Argon of Persia, had a wife who died. She left a request to her husband on her deathbed. "If you ever loved me," she wrote, "then when you remarry, choose only a wife who is a descendant of my own family from China."

Since Argon felt duty bound, he sent three barons to China to escort a new wife home. They carried letters to the Great Khan requesting his help. As usual, the Great Khan performed well. He picked a beautiful, educated, and talented girl named Kagatin.

Kagatin left China with Argon's men, but eight months later they came back to court. Argon's men were no travelers. The normal western routes had been shut off because of local wars. They just couldn't figure out how to get through.

Argon's men are wild to get home. They believe that they cannot ever get there without our help. And of course this is our chance to leave also.

One reason that the Great Khan is so successful is that he can compromise. He understands the situation completely, and he has decided to let us all go together. He is sad to see us go, but we have promised to return to him after visiting our family and friends. The Khan is giving us two golden tablets with his orders inscribed on them. They are passports that will ensure freedom and safety for all of us through his vast lands. We are now the Khan's ambassadors to the Pope and to the great rulers of Europe.

The great Khan has given us ships and men and provisions enough for two years along with many valuable presents. But his greatest gift is that he is letting us go.

Java Minor
A.D. 1294

𝕯ear Diary,

Oh, I can tell astounding stories about Sumatra. There are brown, hairy animals here which have faces that look like humans! They have hands and feet like humans, too, though they do not walk upright. They are called monkeys. I can't stop staring at them. I'm waiting for them to talk, but they won't.

*D*ear Diary,

After the three months at sea I feel that we see nothing but water. We're on the Indian Seas now. Blue water, blue skies, stormy water, stormy skies, blue water; endless water; water, water, water.

ear Diary,

Ceylon, the place with the highest of mountains, is said to be the spot where the first man, Adam, is buried.

But whether or not you believe it depends on who you are. If you are a Saracen, which is an Arab or a Muslim, you do believe it's Adam's tomb. If you are a Buddhist, it's another story. Then you believe it's the Buddha's tomb.

What do I think? Marco Polo thinks it's a high mountain and the view from the top is beautiful.

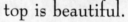ear Diary,

What about India! This land is so vast, the parts are so different from each other, I could fill a whole journal on India alone if I could just make the time to write.

In some parts there are strange people who go around naked in the heat, wearing nothing but valuable jewels.

In Maabar, a province of India, they have beds with curtains which you can close by pulling a string. They are ingenious. The curtains keep out the tarantulas as well as the small harmless bugs, yet because they are made of a light airy material, the breezes can circulate through. This is absolutely necessary because it's so hot here.

*ear Diary,*

You should see the Indian nuts! These are nuts as big as your head, with milk and a sweet wet meat inside! The Venetians won't believe it when I tell them about these coconuts!

In some provinces the people are all black and although they are very dark-skinned naturally, they rub oil of sesame seeds on their children three times a day to make them appear even blacker. They love the look of black skin. They must have thought I was hideously ugly.

*ear Diary,*

Land!

We have finally reached Argon's court, but Argon is dead. Argon's son has received Kagatin, and he is grateful to us for her. We are to be his guests while we regain our strength. In addition, he has given us another set of passports to freedom: four heavy golden tablets inscribed with promises of protection.

Dear Diary,

Bad news today. Messengers have come with news from China telling of the Great Khan's death. I am so sad to hear about our dear friend. But now I have to make a confession which I am almost embarrassed to admit. There is a good side to this misfortune as well. Now we're free to stay in Venice forever.

Dear Diary,

Farewell to Argon's son. Good-bye to Kagatin. We're on the way to Trebizond and Constantinople. It won't be long now.
Destination: Venice! I can hardly wait!

Dear Diary,

As we sail into the Grand Canal after twenty-four years, the pink and yellow buildings catch the sunlight to welcome us. I never want to leave Venice again.
Thanks be to God that we returned safely to the country of my birth.
Long live Venice!
I believe it was God's pleasure that we should get back in order that people might learn about the things that the world contains. Thanks be to God!

Just before Marco Polo was born in 1254 in Venice, his father Nicolo and his uncle Maffeo, who were both merchants, left on a trading trip which took them all the way to China. Since his mother died when he was very young, Marco Polo was raised by other relatives. He was also trained to be a merchant.

In 1269 Nicolo and Maffeo returned to Venice. They intended to go back to China immediately at the invitation of the Mongol ruler of Asia, the Kublai Khan. The Khan was interested in the Polos personally but also in Christianity. The Khan was tolerant of and curious about all religions. He asked the Polos to bring back missionaries from the Pope who might introduce Christianity to Asia.

However, since the Pope had died the Polos had to wait for the new Pope to be chosen. In addition, it was difficult to find missionaries willing to travel so far. But by 1271 they were ready to leave. This time they decided to let Marco come with them.

The three Polos sailed from Venice to Acre, a seaport in the Holy Land. After stopping in Jerusalem, they rode camels in caravans past Mount Ararat in Armenia, past Saba in Persia, now Iran, all the way to Hormuz, a Persian seaport on the Gulf of Oman. They wanted to continue by sea, but they could not find seaworthy ships, so they continued by camel caravan. They had their difficulties.

They crossed high mountains, including the Pamir Pass in Afghanistan and vast deserts, including the Gobi in Mongolia. Once, when Marco got sick, they had to stop to wait for him to recover, which added a whole year to the trip. Finally they arrived in Shangdu, China, the Khan's summer palace, in 1274.

The Kublai Khan was delighted. He welcomed them like brothers. By 1275 Marco Polo was becoming fluent in the local languages. He had been to Kanbalu, now Beijing, China, and he had grown accustomed to many of the new things which had so amazed him at first. After a short time the Khan sent him on many missions through eastern and southern China as his ambassador, as well as to Burma, Indochina, the Indonesian islands, and Malaya. The Khan's land holdings were so vast that he could not oversee them properly by himself. He enjoyed the acute observations Marco Polo brought back from these visits. As an additional

Marco Polo's Journey

mark of honor, the Khan appointed Marco Polo as governor of Yang-Gui, now Yang-Chou, China, for three years.

But finally, after many years, the Polo family began to think of going home. The Khan would have liked them to stay in China forever. This was a problem because the Polos realized they could never get home without the Khan's blessing. Traveling was dangerous. They needed protection from the Khan.

In 1291 the Polos found their opportunity to leave. A Persian ruler, the Khan's relative, sent for a Chinese bride. The escort party was unable to make the trip back to Persia. They had tried but failed because it was too difficult. When the Polos offered to deliver the bride on their way home, the Khan sadly agreed.

It was 1291 when the Polos sailed from Zayton, now Chuan-Chou, in Southern China. Their route took them south of Singapore, north of Java Minor, now Sumatra, to Ceylon, now Sri Lanka, around the tip of India, across the Arabian Sea, into the Gulf of Oman and back to Hormuz in Persia. They delivered the bride there and continued over land, probably on camels, all the way to Trebizond, now Trabzon, Turkey, on the Black Sea. They crossed the Black Sea by ship to Constantinople, now Istanbul, Turkey, and continued by ship to Venice.

It was 1295, twenty-four years after they had left. They had traveled almost fifteen thousand miles.

The Polos returned to find Venice and its neighboring city of Genoa at war. Marco Polo joined this war. He commanded Venetian ships against the Genoese, but in 1296 he was captured and jailed in Genoa. From prison Marco Polo sent for the logs of his journeys. Using his old notebook for reference, he dictated *The Travels of Marco Polo* to his cellmate, a man named Rustichiello, who was a professional writer. By the time they were released in 1298, the book was finished.

Description of the World or *The Travels of Marco Polo* tells all of Marco Polo's stories and undoubtedly a few extras too. It is still the most famous travel book in the world.

Generations of explorers have been inspired by Marco Polo's descriptions. Scholars have proven many of even the most extraordinary parts of the book to be true. And even now, in the age of easy air travel and space exploration, the book is fascinating to read.